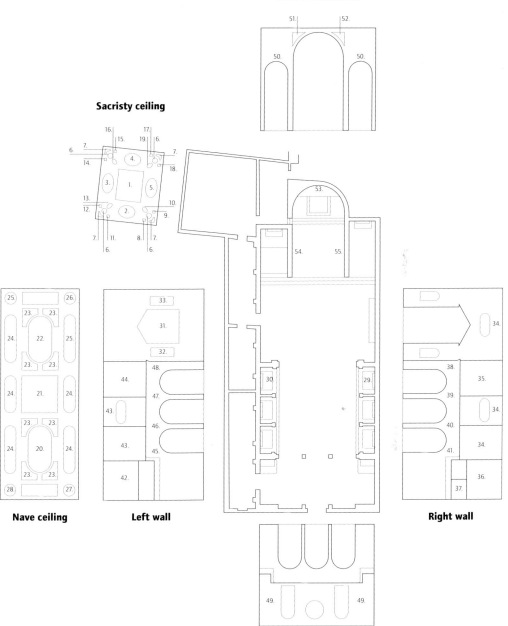

Arch of main altar

Sacristy ceiling

Nave ceiling

Left wall

Right wall

Inner facade

Veronese

in the church of San Sebastiano

by
Augusto Gentili
Michele Di Monte

Chorus Marsilio

THE WORKS
OF VERONESE

SACRISTY

Ceiling
1. Coronation of the Virgin
2. St John the Evangelist
3. St Mathew
4. St Mark
5. St Luke
6. Four tondi with cherubs
7. Four Cardinal Virtues
8. Judith and Holofernes
9. Abraham and Melchisedech
10. The Creation of Eve
11. Esther and Ahasuerus
12. Moses receiving the tablets
13. Eviction from the Garden of Eden
14. David and Goliath
15. The Judgement of Solomon
16. Discovery of the original sin
17. Cain and Abel
18. Moses prayer during the battle against Amalek
19. The original sin

NAVE

Ceiling
The Stories of Esther
20. Repudiation of Vashti
21. Esther crowned by Ahasuerus
22. Triumph of Mordechai
23. Angels supporting the frames
24. Decorations with flowers and fruit
25. Hope
26. Charity
27. Faith
28. Justice

Third side chapel on the right
29. Crucifixion

Grimani chapel
30. Virgin and Child, St Catherine and Brother Michele Spaventi

31. **Organ**
Presentation of Jesus at the Temple
(*doors closed*)
The Pool of Bethesda
(*doors open*)
Nativity
Figures of Virtues
32. Isaiah
33. David

Frescoes on the right wall
34. Solomonic column frieze with figures of Prophets and Sibyls
35. St Sebastian pierced by the arrows
36. St Sebastian before Diocletian
37. Monk leaving the choir
38. St Luke
39. St Mathew
40. St Thomas
41. Apostle with scroll

Frescoes on the left wall
42. Martyrdom of St Sebastian
43. Solomonic column frieze with figures of Prophets and Sibyls
44. Three archers
45. St John the Evangelist
46. St James
47. St Andrew
48. St Peter

Frescoes on the inner facade
49. Solomonic column frieze with figures of Prophets and Sibyls

Arch frescoes on main altar
50. Solomonic column frieze with figures of Prophets and Sibyls
51. Announcing Angel
52. Announced Virgin

Chancel
53. Virgin and Child in Glory with Saints Sebastian, Peter, Catherine and Francis
54. Saints Mark and Marcellian being led to martyrdom
55. Martyrdom of St Sebastian

Introduction

On the site of an oratory dedicated to Our Lady of the Assumption, attached to a modest fourteenth-century Hieronymite monastery, a church was built in the second half of the fifteenth century with the supplementary dedication to St Sebastian, which the legendary saint of the arrows had earned by preserving the inhabitants of the area from the terrible plague of 1464. But before long the spaces of the church and monastery were too small for the needs of the community, so in January 1506 the foundations for a new building were struck, under the direction of Antonio Abbondi, better known as Scarpagnino, to be eventually concluded with its severe facade only in 1548.

In 1542 the prior of the Hieronymite order, Bernardo Torlioni from

Verona, called on Scarpagnino to alter the plan for the reconstruction and restructuring of the church before completion with the insertion of six chapels, three on each side, inside the nave. The intention was evidently to ensure the convent coffers an unprecedented flow of money. No papal indulgence, no appeal to devotion and piety could stimulate the generosity of the faithful like the right of burial. Many illustrious Venetian families were ready to finance the construction of their own chapel, to furnish, endow and decorate their altars and to generously contribute to the works of the church and monastery, provided they knew that the monks would eternally celebrate mass on their behalf and pray for the welfare of their souls.

Given that in 1542 the church was almost finished and there were no urgent works in progress, this search for new funds suggests that Torlioni was already thinking about the expensive job of decorating the entire church. Construction of the side chapels not only determined the current appearance of the church from an architectural point of view, it also created the financial resources allowing it to become one of the most representative examples of the work of Paolo Veronese, who transformed Scarpagnino's sober structure into a rich, connected and colourful whole with his paintings and his real and artificial architecture.

The start of Veronese's work at San Sebastiano squared perfectly with the conclusion of the side chapels. In August 1554, the patrician Marcantonio Grimani, who had been the first to secure one of the new chapels, accepted the prior's invitation to take on the cost of completing the last two, which had remained without patrons after the others had been assigned. With his finances now clearly in credit, Torlioni could focus decisively on achieving his final aim and, between the end of 1554 and the beginning of 1555, called his young fellow countryman to paint the canvases for the ceiling of the sacristy. Veronese, who had come to Venice a couple of years earlier, had not only acquired a substantial figurative training in the city and in his city of origin, between architectural classicism (San-

5

micheli) and pictorial mannerism (Correggio, Parmigianino, Giulio Romano), he also had the right 'political' relations with the grand families, and was still at work in the Doge's Palace decorating the ceilings of the three rooms belonging to the Council of the Ten.

The decoration of the sacristy

On 8 March 1546 Maestro Luca *marangon* (builder) received the balance owing from Bernardo Torlioni for the wooden furnishings of the sacristy: the ceiling, the closets, the pews and two walnut doors. The craftsman did not build a complete ceiling, but a big multiple setting, where the various, differently shaped and sized spaces could have no other purpose than to house paintings: the prior had evidently already conceived the ambitious pictorial project for the sacristy.

But new works did not go ahead for several years. The sacristy came into focus again only in October 1555 with the finishing and decorative work carried out by Maestro Bartolomeo da Bologna *indorador* (gilder). The big setting was now finally ready to house the paintings by Paolo Veronese, which at that date must have almost been finished. Indeed, by 23 November 1555, as inscribed on the book held by one of the cherubs in the side tondi, all the canvases had been inserted in their respective frames and the sacristy could be said to be definitively complete.

Maestro Luca had left a big rectangular, almost square space at the centre of the ceiling, surrounded by four irregular spaces that were also rectangular but long and low with their short sides rounded. The celebration of the *Coronation of the Virgin* was placed in the central space, to fine effect, immediately resuming the original Marian dedication of the church. The four evangelists, shown in the canvases in the side spaces, are rather forced by the anomalous shape of their sections to adopt poses that only the mastery of Paolo Veronese could manage to make seem natural. Four other round frames towards the corners are reserved for canvases with pairs of cherubs, in turn also fairly cramped in their narrow space.

The *Coronation of the Virgin* takes place in the glory of the sky, on a special stand of vaporous clouds, with a complete manifestation of the trinity and some angels flying in a blaze of light. The evangelists appear with books and their usual attributes. Two pairs of cherubs carry stones with inscriptions that repeatedly invite Mary to accept glorification. The other two carry, respectively, a large book, the Old Testament (with the date of the work: 23 November 1555) and a smaller one, the New Testament. In order to contemplate and celebrate the event, and therefore to come as close to heaven as possible, the evangelists and cherubs are placed on top of the symbolic mountain.

Several other scenes around the tondi, evidently decided later and plausibly entrusted to assistants, are painted in chiaroscuro directly onto the wooden ceiling. The story of the ancestors, which usefully

Coronation of the Virgin, 1555
sacristy ceiling

introduces the traditional concept of Mary/new Eve, appears in the four ovals towards the corners of the central section. In the corners of the ceiling are the *Four Cardinal Virtues*, also traditionally incorporated into the virtues of Mary, together with that of humility, which is also the distinctive characteristic of her pose and attitude in the glorious moment of the *Coronation*. Two stories from the Old Testament stand at the side of each *Virtue* (*David and Goliath* and the *Judgement of Solomon* beside *Temperance*; *Moses' prayer during the battle against Amalek* and *Cain and Abel* beside *Prudence*; *Abraham and Melchisedech* and *Judith and Holofernes* beside *Strength*; *Moses receiving the tablets* and *Esther before Ahasuerus* beside *Justice*): arranged, as can be seen, in a fairly disordered way compared to the usual interpretative associations between two episodes and/or between individual episode and individual Virtue. All this shows that the pictorial decoration was only organised after the building of the wooden ceiling, and was materially and thematically developed from the *Coronation*, though without a defined and detailed programme – unless at some indeterminable time the panels have not been moved (though the inference remains difficult to verify), altering the original position of the stories. This question remains open – though for another time – to the prospect of a more consistent reconstruction. We have no doubts at present, though, in sustaining that the *Coronation* has at some stage been remounted back to front: it is unthinkable that one should have to cross the room and stand against the back wall in order to view it from the right side.

Finally, the highly interesting series of stories from the Old Testament (*Sacrifice of Isaac, Jacob's Dream and Jacob's fight with the Angel, The Parting of the Red Sea*) and the New (*Nativity, Baptism, Praying in the Garden* and *Resurrection of Christ*) has now been returned to the walls of the sacristy after years of absence and long restoration. Apparently all without documentation, these have been arranged in a fairly improbable sequence (and complicated by the presence of some other paintings that are visibly extraneous to the series). They are attributed without much support to a group of painters that is not particularly united if the name of Marten de Vos should appear alongside that of Bonifacio de' Pitati, his workshop (all to be reconstructed) and that of Antonio Palma. We will reconsider this when there has been time to study them further.

Tondo with cherubs, 1555
sacristy ceiling

Ceiling of the nave: *The Stories of Esther*

Paolo Veronese painted the three big nave ceiling pictures with stories from the Book of Esther, the Jewish heroine who saved her people from the fury of the Persian King Ahasuerus and the intrigues of his minister Haman, between 1 December 1555 (date of the contract with Bernardo Torlioni) and 31 October 1556 (date of the final payment).

The first scene is that of the *Repudiation of Vashti*, the queen guilty of not responding to the king's commandment to attend his banquet. Deprived of her crown, Vashti is forced to go down the steps of a staircase that is certainly not a monumental one, almost a service exit, accompanied by the young figure of ignorance with the grotesque face of pride.

In the central picture with *Esther crowned by Ahasuerus*, the young beauty, chosen from all as the new queen, wins the crown from the king which Vashti had lost. Dressed up and adorned as a Venetian bride, she is accompanied by the handmaidens of chastity and humility, and can climb the high marble steps of the solemn throne, kneeling before her lord. On the right, the presence of the dreadful Haman, showing off in his shining armour and in the company of a deformed courtesan, announces the threat to exterminate the Jewish people and the subsequent events.

The concluding painting is that of the *Triumph of Mordechai*, servant at the door of the royal palace, adoptive father of Esther and instigator of her work to convince Ahasuerus to save the Jews. The Persian king, discovering in the chronicles that Mordechai had in his turn overturned a conspiracy to kill him, though without receiving any thanks, orders Haman to dress him as a prince, with crown and sceptre, and to honour him with a horse parade in the city square. Even though the Bible story does not include anything of the sort, in the extreme glimpse shown by Veronese, the splendid white horse of the very calm Mordechai seems to stop at the last moment before the chasm, with the aid of two practical soldiers, while Haman's uncontrolled black horse is on the point of falling along with its agitated rider: once again there are those who ascend and those who descend, those who are diminished and those who are exalted. Heads and hands wave on the balcony, the red standard with the black eagle waves in the sky.

Given that Esther is regularly seen in the Christian analysis as prefiguring the Virgin, it is evident that the coronation at the centre of the nave ceiling is connected to the coronation in the sacristy ceiling. It is a narrative conclusion – but anticipated in the executive programme – to the uninterrupted sequence on the co-redeeming function of Mary seen almost everywhere, from the *Sibyls* and *Prophets* on the walls, to the *Annunciation* in the triumphal arch, the *Nativity* and the *Presentation of Jesus at the Temple* in the organ, the *Assumption* (no longer here) in the chancel dome, and through to the apparition in glory of the Virgin and Child in the main altarpiece.

Repudiation of Vashti, 1556
nave ceiling

Esther crowned by Ahasuerus, 1556
nave ceiling

Triumph of Mordechai, 1556
nave ceiling

The controversial anti-Protestant aspect usually recognised in all these representations of Mary is obvious and inevitable in years that run parallel to the Council of Trent and its doctrinal and normative results. Indeed, this is so fully acquired and implicit that it does not even amount to a meaning but only a very general contextual frame, though one lacking in substantial connections with a selection and definition of the stories of Esther *in images*, which excludes her prefigurative role as mediator. Exactly the same thing is true of the bland and discounted political allusions that can be read, if desired, in the layers of equivalence accumulated on the figure of Esther (= Virgin, Venice, Queen), or in the imperial eagle on Mordechai's standard.

Taking inspiration from the medieval and humanist comments on the Book of Esther, Bernardo Torlioni and Paolo Veronese ordered the sequence of the three paintings on the thematic move from Fortune to Providence: if the casual and voluble Fortune brings to the throne the haughty Vashti, if she allows the wicked Haman to prepare the destruction of the Jews with the approval of a distracted and moody sovereign and if she humiliates the excellent Mordechai in a subordinate role, then the targeted and constant Providence punishes the quarrelsome queen and the criminal minister, exalts the humble, obedient girl, saves the chosen people and acknowledges the leader with due honours. All this is possible within a moral and theological conception that calls for the intervention of mercy in exclusive support of personal virtues, of the commitment and even risk in the works. All this is represented – also exploiting the impervious location to the maximum advantage – contrasting ascent and descent in the paintings, high and low, salvation and damnation. There is then the addition of ingenious metaphoric solutions to apparently only material problems: such as the one that allows the observer to see Esther and Mordechai while walking along the nave toward the chancel, but which then, in order to see Vashti being driven out, forces one to turn one's back on the altar.

If this is the main theme, the meaning (or overall reasons and functions) refers as always directly to the specific context, to the historic reality of the place and the moment, to the people involved and who dictate it. In 1538, after a long period of serious moral and disciplinary disorder between the Hieronymite order, Pope Paul III had launched an interdict against the church and monastery of San Sebastiano, and at the beginning of the following year nominated Bernardo Torlioni as vicar-general, charging him with reforming the rules of the congregation. By 1541 the new constitution was ready and at the end of the year the interdict was lifted. In 1542 Torlioni was called to the priorship of San Sebastiano. It can therefore be appreciated that the project for the six new chapels launched by Torlioni precisely in 1542 was closely related to his moralising and reorganising work, aimed at recovering spiritual and material credit for the monastery after the collapse of its image during the years of crisis.

Choosing precisely those three moments from the Biblical story for Paolo Veronese, Bernardo Torlioni built the exaltation of the event and of his role on the Christian interpretation. After having chased out the disobedient and rebellious elements with Vashti, he could finally consign to Esther the crown of renewed authority. He reserved for himself the figure of Mordechai, Esther's (the Church's) wise guide, the main figure in the deliverance of his people (of the Church): in a word, the perfect model of an excellent prelate.

The side chapels

The six side chapels were completed without much haste between 1544 and 1553 on the model of the two alongside the main one, completed some time earlier. The most historically and artistically important was the first one assigned (30 January 1544), the third on the left, being that of Marcantonio Grimani. He was the main financier of the whole project and wanted to add his own proud portrait and the full-figure ones of his two eponymous saints *Mark* and *Antony Abbot*, all signed by Alessandro Vittoria, to the rich marble

Virgin and Child, St Catherine and Brother Michele Spaventi, 1578-80
Grimani chapel

ornaments and magniloquent sepulchral stone. They were joined by the chiaroscuri depicting the *Praying in the Garden* and the *Deposition in the Sepulchre* alongside the *Kiss of Judah* in the vault and the *Resurrection* on the back wall, all to be attributed without any doubt to the late career of the great and neglected Andrea Schiavone. The graceful, pious painting by Paolo Veronese showing the *Virgin and Child, St Catherine and Brother Michele Spaventi* now stands on the altar, in an absurd arrangement that in a single blow spoils the marble harmony of the chapel and conceals the chromatic harmonies of the painting.

The other two chapels on the left were built last (1552-3) under the direction of the monastery, but financed later by a large donation from Marcantonio Grimani. The first was conceded to Vincenzo Pellegrini on 24 June 1557. The owner's surname is enough to explain the rare iconography of the altarpiece painted by Andrea Schiavone: *Christ and two disciples are walking toward Emmaus*, so all three are pilgrims. There is no other information on the second chapel; on the altar there is a *Baptism of Christ* from the Veronese school, not in the least insignificant and plausibly attributed to Benedetto Caliari.

The three chapels on the right are the result of the intermediate stage of enlargement and concession works following the Grimani 'prototype'. The third was assigned on 14 December 1544 to the noble Gerolamo Garzoni; on the altar a *Crucifixion* of splendid simplicity – painted by Paolo Veronese at a time decidedly prior to 1560-65 against cur-

Crucifixion, 1560-65
third side chapel on the right

rent hypotheses – in which the wood literally crosses the belly of the fainted Mary, who thus becomes mother of the Cross, the direct origin of the path of redemption. The second, conceded at an imprecise time in 1546 to the jurist Melio da Cortona, renowned for having left an *Annunciation* by Titian to the Scuola Grande di San Rocco, has the delightful marble group of the *Virgin and Child with the Infant St John* by Tomaso Lombardo, signed and dated 1577. In the first, assigned to Paolo Onorati by 1550, the otherwise excellent altarpiece by Federico Bencovich dedicated to the *Blessed Pietro Gambacorta of Pisa*, founder of the Hieronymite order, which towards 1725-30 replaced a *Nativity* by Giovan Battista Zelotti, clashes considerably in such a sixteenth-century context.

The decoration of the organ

Bernardo Torlioni commissioned the organ in October 1558 from Alessandro Visentin and its casing from Maestro Domenico da Treviso, who agreed to follow Paolo Veronese's special design. Maestro Francesco Fiorentino and Maestro Bartolomeo Bolognese were then respectively appointed to carry out the carving and gilding. The structure of the organ was also required to balance the enormous sepulchre for the archbishop Livio Podacataro designed by Jacopo Sansovino, being built on the front wall, at the same time acting as a model for the overall layout. In addition to the *Nativity* on the parapet, Paolo also painted the big doors between 1559 and 1560, which when closed show the *Presentation of Jesus at the Temple*, in a solemn but not particularly innovative manner, and when open a very original version of the *Pool of Bethesda*. On the right, the healed paralytic, with paradoxically athletic physique and still-suffering face, is getting ready, as suggested by Christ, to take up his pallet and go; further back there is a black man with a fanciful hat, along with a young man lifted up from a pool that is not there. Various people are waiting on the left, now looking toward the giant cripple who has noticed what is happening on the other side and is pointing to gain attention; the angel, which should descend to move the waters, is actually falling headlong from the sky, showing the divine cause of the event. The pool, as noted, is not there, even though we can imagine it below. This is evidently not only an expedient to simplify the layout but mainly to emphasise the new miracle, which literally cancels the presumed pagan magic of the invisible waters. The spiritual redemption as a final result of the material healing carried out by Christ is sealed in the organ decoration by the role of co-redemption played by Mary, made tangible in the *Nativity* and developed in the *Presentation* on the threshold between temple and church, between ancient and new law.

The decoration of the organ
doors, 1559-60
centre: *Presentation of Jesus
at the Temple* (doors closed);
at the sides: *The Pool of
Bethesda* (doors open)

The wall frescoes

The Hieronymite fathers wanted to devote a decorative programme to St Sebastian, to whom the church was co-dedicated, which by extension, richness and articulation would recall the more monumental legendary cycles of late-medieval style. But the overall arrangement and choices are all new, especially taking into account the iconographic tradition by which the saint had been portrayed in Venetian churches prior to the task entrusted to Veronese. In the mid-sixteenth century, the typical and popularly circulated image of Sebastian in Venice was still that based on the Bellini model, and on the parallel versions by Mantegna and Antonello. These showed the young, half-naked martyr pierced by arrows, solitary and impassive, projected onto the background of the noetic space of the polyptych or contained, more or less as co-figure, in the liturgical one of the altarpiece, as could be seen, for example, in the Chiesa della Carità, that of San Zanipolo or that of San Giobbe. Titian, too, in 1522 had held to the fairly dominant type of the enthralled and injured saint for the Averoldi polyptych in Brescia, though with more realistic pathos and more patent Christological allusions.

When, however, Paolo Veronese prepared to paint the frescoes for the upper tier of the nave walls in March 1558, on the side of the monks' choir – in agreement with and under the guidance of his faithful patron, the prior Bernardo Torlioni – the painter had quite a different programme in mind. The first of the stories of Sebastian unfolds in the renewed and extended space of the choir, arranged in a U-shape above the side chapels and along the inner facade. Here the saint is not evoked, or better invoked, primarily as the hieratic thaumaturge, protector against the plague, but is mainly the hero of the action in which he figures. Veronese, in effect, did not refrain from contemplating the more usual and traditional image, but also inserted him in a complex context of references and relations. The martyr thus appears, with statuesque composure, between the majestic Solomonic columns that mark the wall decorations, in line with the right end of the choir (looking toward the main altar), to counterpoint and almost proleptically 'perfect' the non-Biblical and Old Testament series of sibyls and prophets that face one another along the perimeter of the nave. On the other hand, however, the figure is not reduced to an abstract presence in the symbolic and cultural order, but introduces a more dynamic and engaging narrative dimension that symmetrically involves the figures of the archers on the opposite wall intent on targeting the martyr – three, as many as there are darts that have

Three archers, 1558 c.
fresco on the left wall

already hit Sebastian – and spreads out the action so empirically as to actually put us within the range of their trajectory.

It is thus also a concrete representation of the well-known episode of the transverberation, which however is not the final act of Sebastian's gesture, but rather foreshadows the subsequent more animated developments Veronese put into images according to a well-designed staging. Regarding the sources for this, painter and patron could have made use of the Latin *Passio* traditionally attributed to St

St Sebastian pierced by the arrows, 1558
fresco on the right wall

Ambrose, or the version updated by Jacopo da Varagine in the *Golden Legend* or, more easily still, one of the various vernacular editions of the latter. A large picture opens up on the right wall of the choir space itself, above the stalls, showing a scene in which the young soldier – believed dead after the torture of the arrows, but rather tended by the pious Irene and who has miraculously recovered his health – confronts no lesser person than the Emperor Diocletian to reproach him for the persecutions against the Christians. Veronese underscored the connection of the narrative sequence – note the direction of the saint's firm step and the 'memento' of the arrow in his left hand – and at the same time noted the representative register deviation, framing the 'recounted'

story in a decorative frame, a kind of false, rounded off proscenium with festoons and satyresses which he had also adopted in another historical religious painting in the same years, the *Feast in the House of Simon* for the Benedictines of Santi Nazzaro e Celso in Verona. The choice of episode is no mere chance and the deviation also marks an additional value. It is no longer only generically devotional, but more specifically political-historical and ecclesiastical. Sebastian does not so much appear as the saint to be invoked against the plague, and not even as the instrument of healing and conversion which also abound in his *Acta*, but as the incarnation of the ideal of the *miles Christi*, face to face with the incarnation of that imperial and pagan power that the Christian faith, although persecuted, had by now overturned and defeated. It is with good reason that the false statues of Peter and Paul tower over the inner facade, at the sides of the big oculus and the two windows illuminating the choir, alongside the stories of Sebastian, in place of the prophets. They are the pillars of the new church who, like Sebastian, bore testimony to their faith contending in Rome with the emperor and therefore enduring martyrdom, both on the same day.

Consistently, on the left wall, opposite the scene of the *reprehensio*, Veronese portrayed the inevitable outcome of the story, the final torture of the saint inflicted by the emperor himself with the final

order for his body to be thrown into the Cloaca Massima so as not to leave any memory. The victim, tied to a device – in a 'difficult' view, recalling Tintoretto's *Miracle of the Slave* and Titian's more or less contemporary *St Laurence* – is about to be beaten to death with clubs. But already an almost invisible blade of light falls to meet the rapt gaze of Sebastian, while, at bottom left, a young woman peeps out, in open contrast to the ugly faces of the assassins, perhaps alluding to the compassionate Lucina who will collect the remains of the saint to deposit them in the catacombs, as had already been done with the apostles Peter and Paul.

The selection and coordination of the various elements in the decorative programme are thus a knowing and precocious response to the petitions made by a new model of sanctity that was taking shape in the years of the Tridentine council. This was concentrated on the recovery of paleo-Christian sources, perhaps also at the cost of legendary aspects that were dearer to popular devotion, and guided by interests that, if not exactly philological in a strict sense, were at least historical-apologetic and controversial. From this point of view, the *Acta martyrum* are the ideal context for the celebration and relaunch, also figurative, of the Church militant. On the other hand, an emphasis of the especially Roman vocation of the original church could even be consistent with the personal inclinations of Torlioni, who had been directly nominated vicar-general of the order by Paul III in 1539 with a mandate to reform its constitution.

The monks, entering the choir, found themselves immediately faced with the courageous invective of Sebastian who, with calculated rhetorical gesture, almost involuntarily but not fortuitously points

*Martyrdom
of St Sebastian, 1558 c.
fresco on the left wall*

out the false painted door mirroring the real one below the main scene in which the painter depicted one of the Hieronymite fathers making his entry into the choir. Thanks to the interaction of different representative registers, the old story is joined to the modern one and those to whom the images are directed are 'pointed out' as the real heirs of that for which the martyr was in his turn advocate.

The chancel

This admonitory and 'competitive' interpretation of the saintly story is if anything too obvious in the second cycle of paintings Father Torlioni wanted to consecrate to the martyr Sebastian, in the much more prestigious chancel. He again entrusted the work to Veronese, whom he provided with both the design for the altar and the overall spatial arrangement of the main chapel. The canvases were probably painted between 1559 and 1565, and the resumption of the theme is significant, though can also be explained by the simple fact that, then as now, the new frescoes in the choir were not visible from the nave. But the variants are also indicative. Alongside the altarpiece there are two big canvases that show Sebastian encouraging Mark and Marcellian not to deny the Christian faith on the left and, on the right, Sebastian himself at the supreme moment of his martyrdom. Even though the association of the chosen episodes in the first cycle was iconographically already fairly new, the diptych chosen for the chancel must have been even more exceptional. Once again the space qualified by the images is organised thematically and narratively into a unitary logic and the weave of references and responses is tight.

Saints Mark and Marcellian being led to martyrdom, 1565
chancel

Here, too, the cycle takes its cue from the left picture, where the directional impulse is more apparent. The brothers Mark and Marcellian, converts to Christianity, are judged by their faith and forced to choose between recanting or martyrdom. Led in chains from the court of law (note the poor pauper who, as usual, begs at the door of the rich and powerful), they meet their elderly parents on the road who, with their wives and children, try to dissuade them from continuing in their choice, when Sebastian, in shining armour, intervenes, urging his companions rather to endure the final battle with courage. Veronese kept to the sources, but without literal scruples, recombining the narrative sequence and the pertinence of the details to obtain a scene of greater dramatic concentration and clearer thematic evidence, even at the cost, paradoxically, of some less realistic omissions: the guards and soldiers, for example, who should probably be escorting the prisoners, seem too far in the background, but, for reasons of script, room had to be made for the main characters in the episode.

The central theme of the action is the problem of the difficult choice between worldly affections and the call of martyrdom. Sebastian's equally rhetorical gesture is not required here to champion the Christians' cause before the persecutor, as in the choir fresco, but becomes an *exhortatio ad homines*, appealing directly to the neophytes to follow the saint on the path of the supreme sacrifice. The superior value of truth that inspires the call of the *miles christianus* is then attested to literally by the miraculous apparition of the angel with open book in hand, a detail the painter correctly inferred from the text, but functionally altered in context for this different situa-

tion. And the fact that an authentic imitation of Christ is in play, in that he leaves life, is also shown, *e contrario*, by the detail, unusual in a scene of the type, of the monkey on the left which, as is its nature, copies Sebastian's gesture without knowing what it does.

The whole composition is unbalanced and presses toward the outside, to the right, in the direction of the source of light that illuminates the scene and thus, in the real space of the chapel, indicates the main altar. The agitated movement of the lateral paintings is recomposed in the measured contemplative dimension of the altarpiece, where the theme of Sebastian is sealed and ideally culminates in that of the Virgin, who also proceeds from the nave to the apse. Other saints appear in adoration of the Virgin and Child. These are eponymous members of Cataruzza Cornaro's family, who had acquired burial rights in the main chapel: Giovanni, Pietro, Francesco, Caterina and, behind her, another not easily recognisable saint. This latter is often identified as Elisabetta – because of the correspondence of her name with that of Lise Soranzo, Cornaro's acquired granddaughter and testamentary executor – but is qualified here rather as a holy martyr by the palm that appears at her shoulder. The hypothesis reported in the past by Ridolfi, that the painter wanted to create a likeness of his patron Torlioni in the face of Francesco, seems fairly implausible, partly because in 1560 the prior was already over 65 years old.

While respecting the iconographic and compositional conventions dictated by the altarpiece form, Veronese did not, however, refrain from articulating a circumspect hierarchical architecture. The hub of the painted space is the central axis that visually connects the figure of Sebastian with that of Mary, seated on a throne of clouds that almost materially rests (given the projected shadow) on the columns. Along with the arrows, these are an attribute of the young martyr, but possibly also recall Titian's versions in the Pesaro altarpiece at the Frari, not without ulterior allusions toward the immaculate. The obviously angular stone acts as a solid pedestal, on which, not by chance, rest the keys of St Peter, who in turn holds the Bible in his hand. The literally cardinal role of the church of martyrdom as *Ecclesia triumphans* could not be better underscored, even in historic-doctrinal terms. This seems eloquently shown by the somewhat different prominence of space conceded to Sebastian in the chancel, compared to the slightly cramped figures of the saints Paul the Hermit and Onouphrius at the sides of the altar, examples of the ascetic and contemplative ideal that was also institutionally foundational for the Hieronymite order.

But if the main altarpiece represents an ideal end to the figurative programme conceived by Father Torlioni and Paolo Veronese, the narrative climax of the main St Sebastian cycle takes place in the big chancel canvas on the right, which once connected sequentially with its counterpart, and in similar fashion coordinates with the altarpiece and opens finally onto another spatial, figurative and

symbolic dimension. Compared to the equivalent fresco in the choir, the big canvas has a tighter, more compressed composition, in which the rows of numerous onlookers at the torture ritual close up in a narrower, almost claustrophobic space, all in the foreground, and loom over the body of the martyr with a sense of suffocating agitation. The action is carefully studied in detail, because here we are not simply watching a capital execution but, as with the pendant painting, we are witnessing a choice: that of Sebastian, this time, who is the focal point of the story, in the final moment before the martyrdom actually takes place. So it is not so much a display of the sacrifice, as of his reason, because, as Agostino had written in a passage that had taken on great topicality against the background of the sixteenth-century religious crisis, *non poena sed causa martyrem facit*. The executioners, with their stolid expressions, are still preparing for their dreadful task on the right; on the other side a coloured attendant is bringing a bundle of switches that will evidently be used for the purpose. Officials of various rank attend and supervise the macabre ritual, displaying royal insignia. The double-headed, crowned eagle stands out in the foreground at left, while gilt lilies can be seen on the opposite side and, as usual, the turbans of exotic dignitaries also appear. Closer to Sebastian are the highest priests who, in dazzling clothes, vainly try to convince the young soldier to renounce his faith and sacrifice to the gods: even the statue from high on its pedestal seems to direct an extreme invitation to the martyr. But he has by now taken off his worldly clothes, his cuirass lies at his feet like an empty shell, the inert and ephemeral remains of the *homo vetus*, while the new man aims elsewhere, where his

forefinger and gaze direct, giving complete sense to the peremptory gesture he turned to Mark and Marcellian in the opposite canvas. The lighting, too, which again comes from the main altar side, participates in this dramatic dialectic: the radiant surge that falls beyond the group of figures wisely profiled in backlight and then sweeps over the proscenium makes the contrast stand out forcefully between the idolatrous minister, who with his hood falling over his eyes turns his shoulder to the light source, projecting his shadow of death over the saint, and the illuminated face of Sebastian. As in the choir fresco, his eyes have already been enraptured by the celestial ray that cleaves the scene from on high; but here, not by chance, the martyr also openly invites us to share his vision.

Unfortunately we can now only imagine that spectacle, but until the early eighteenth century, when work had to be done to rebuild the chapel roof, the observer, on reaching the end of the nave, could raise his eyes like Sebastian and discover in the space of the dome the frescoes in which Veronese had portrayed the assumption of the Virgin with God the Father surrounded by angels, the evangelists (in the lunettes) and the fathers of the Church (in the pendentives). With this complex iconographic 'system', the space of the main altar chapel became a synthesis and a completion of the entire figurative path that enlivens the decoration of the whole church. The figures of the Church *ex gentibus* symbolised by the sibyls and that of the Church *ex Synagoga* announced by the prophets, are given form, through incarnation, in the Church of Christ which symbolically triumphs in the Assumption of the Virgin, as they are given form and continue to be given form in history, thanks to the vocation and exemplary testimony of saints and martyrs. But the decoration of the chancel is also the recapitulation and climax of Veronese's painting, of his capacity for visual synthesis, thematic, spatial and scenographic coordination, which connects and extends the architectural, plastic and figurative dimension in what could be defined as a 'fine compound' that was perhaps never to be seen again in Venice as it was in the church of San Sebastiano.

Essential bibliography

TERISIO PIGNATTI, *Le pitture di Paolo Veronese nella chiesa di San Sebastiano*, Milan, Ricordi, 1966.

MADLYN KAHR, *The Meaning of Veronese's Paintings in the Church of San Sebastiano in Venice*, in 'Journal of the Warburg and Courtauld Institutes', XXXIII, 1970, pp. 235-247.

ANTONIO NIERO, *Il programma teologico di Paolo Veronese in San Sebastiano*, in *Da Tiziano a El Greco. Per la storia del Manierismo a Venezia, 1540-1590*, exhibition catalogue (Venice, Palazzo Ducale, September-December 1981), Milan, Electa, 1981, pp. 327-329.

ADRIANA AUGUSTI RUGGERI and SIMONA SAVINI BRANCA, *Chiesa di San Sebastiano: arte e devozione*, Venice, Marsilio, 1994.

TERISIO PIGNATTI and FILIPPO PEDROCCO, *Veronese*, 2 vol., Milan, Electa, 1995.

MICHELE DI MONTE, *La morte bella. Il martirio nella pittura di Tiziano, Tintoretto e Veronese*, in 'Venezia Cinquecento', IX/17, 1999, pp. 91-179.

ANDREAS PRIEVER, *Veronese*, Köln, Könemann, 2000.

PAOLA RANIERI, *La chiesa di San Sebastiano a Venezia: la rifondazione cinquecentesca e la cappella di Marcantonio Grimani*, in 'Venezia Cinquecento', XII/24, 2002, pp. 5-00, with documentary appendices, pp. 89-139.

Translated by
David Graham

Photographs
Cameraphoto Arte, Venice

cover
Paolo Veronese, *Virgin and Child
with Saints Sebastian, Peter, Catherine
and Francis*, 1560-62, detail
Venice, church of San Sebastiano, chancel

© 2005 by Chorus, Venice
© 2005 by Marsilio Editori® s.p.a.
in Venice
First edition: March 2005
ISBN 88-317-8727-6

www.marsilioeditori.it

Printed by
La Grafica & Stampa s.r.l., Vicenza
for Marsilio Editori®, Venice

EDITION   YEAR

10 9 8 7 6 5 4 3 2 1   2005 2006 2007 2008 2009